#jeremiahspeaks

Supporting and Embracing Families with Autism

A 40-day Prayer Journey

Karla Allen

#jeremiahspeaks

FRESH REIGN PUBLISHING
www.freshreign.com

Social Media:
https://facebook.com/FreshReignPublishing/
https://twitter.com/Fresh_Reign
https://instagram.com/karlaallen_

All rights reserved. No part of this book may be reproduced or transmitted in any form or by any means without written permission from the author.

Copyright © 2019 Karla Allen
All rights reserved.
ISBN: 978-0-9854480-2-8

#JEREMIAHSPEAKS

DEDICATION

This book is inspired by and dedicated to my nephew. You are a sign and a wonder. Before you ever spoke in reality, God allowed us to hear you speaking in our dreams. The dreams are now a reality, and I know one day you will stand before thousands to tell your story, in your words, with your voice to **Speak** of God's Grace, Power, and Favor on your life. **Speak**, Prophet J., **Speak**!

According to autisspeaks.org, 1/3 of people with autism are nonverbal. This book is dedicated to the *1/3* and their families. Who can comprehend the dimensions of God's love? His love extends beyond every spectrum, range, distribution, and classification. His love is unlimited and thereby reaches beyond every limitation to touch and heal. May you find comfort, peace, encouragement, and healing as you pray these prayers in faith.

To my family, this is our legacy. God hears and answers prayers.

CONTENTS

Foreword	xi
Acknowledgments	xix
Introduction	Xxi
Day 1	1
Day 2	3
Day 3	5
Day 4	7
Day 5	9
Day 6	11
Day 7	13
Day 8	15
Day 9	17
Day 10	19
Day 11	21
Day 12	23
Day 13	25
Day 14	27
Day 15	29
Day 16	31
Day 17	33
Day 18	35
Day 19	37
Day 20	39
Day 21	41
Day 22	43
Day 23	45
Day 24	47
Day 25	49
Day 26	51
Day 27	53
Day 28	55
Day 29	57
Day 30	59

Day 31...	61
Day 32...	63
Day 33...	65
Day 34...	67
Day 35...	69
Day 36...	71
Day 37...	73
Day 38...	75
Day 39...	77
Day 40...	79
Appendix...	83
About the Author..	87

#JEREMIAHSPEAKS

KARLA ALLEN

FOREWORD

By Radha Richmond and Sarah Morgan

RADHA RICHMOND

Autism is a neurodevelopmental disorder, which can affect communication skills (language development as well as the functional use of said language in social situations), social skills, cognition, gross and fine motor skills, and sensory needs (which can vary). Autism is considered to be on a spectrum, as the impact that it has on each individual varies greatly, and the characteristics exhibited by the individual beyond the language and social deficits can vary. No two individuals with autism are exactly alike. Despite these differences, some things remain the same, and those are the areas in which it impacts the individual. What varies is the extent to which each is affected as well as the needs of each individual within those areas. Additionally, individuals diagnosed with autism whose cognitive development is lower are often considered to have more severe needs in all of the areas due to the combined impact of lower cognitive development and the characteristics associated with the autism diagnosis as well.

In a time where the prevalence of Autism is at an all-time high, and more and more families are being affected by this neurodevelopmental disorder, the church can no longer afford to ignore the needs of its congregants impacted by this disability. Over the past decade, the number of children diagnosed with autism has risen 175% and is now at 1 in 59 children born will have autism (www.autismspeaks.org). Boys are impacted more than girls, with there being a 1:5 ratio of autism diagnosis for girls to boys. In California, there are 112,316 students with autism in the public school system. Schools, medical institutions, and state and community agencies are struggling to keep up with the need given these high numbers, as more research and information is available, and more families are seeking support for their children at an early age. As the first wave of individuals with autism are becoming adults, and looking long term, the fact that these high numbers of children diagnosed with autism eventually are going to become adults who need to be integrated into the community and given tools and skills to pursue higher education and employment, the focus on inclusivity is becoming more of the norm.

Statistics aside, the human impact of this disability is real, and the toll it takes on families in terms of the day to day struggles and triumphs are real as well. For every milestone that a typically developing student achieves, most of the time with little to no direct teaching of that skill on the part of the parents, the student with autism achieves through concentrated, explicit effort on the part of the parent as well as other professionals who may be working with that child. That added effort and the cost in terms of parent time and labor is often lost or not understood by those who do not have students with disabilities. This is where the church family can be of most support to families, coming alongside them with resources, care and understanding, parent education, parent counseling, parent support groups, and programs that are inclusive of students with autism such as vacation bible school, Sunday school, youth groups, etc. In addition to these supports, targeted prayer supports that are connected to the real needs of both the individual with autism and the family supporting that individual are needed.

That's why this book, #jeremiahspeaks, Karla has written, is essential and groundbreaking because it serves to bridge the gap between the faith community and the families that are served within that community who are struggling with this very real-life issue. The families that I have worked with over the past decade, who have children with autism, all go through a similar path in terms of their experiences in learning of this disorder. First, there is the struggle within themselves to seek help as they can tell something is not quite right with their child, then there is inevitable grief in finding out that they have a child with autism, in terms of not knowing what that means long term for their child. There is a process of possibly letting go of some of the dreams that they had for their child as they learn more about the disability. Then, eventually, there is acceptance and peace as they come to understand the disorder as well as come to understand their own child's specific strengths and weaknesses, their personality, and their beauty. This is another crucial area of support for families, where faith in God can have such a tremendous positive impact, giving the peace that only God can provide, and giving the hope that only God gives, having faith that their child has a destiny, a purpose beyond that which they can see or understand. This is what can get a family through some tough times and keep them persevering through obstacles.

    The reason why I characterize some of these situations as challenging. Because, in a practical sense, they are. Having to directly teach a child basic skills that other children learn naturally through their environment without a lot of explicit instruction is difficult, not easy. The isolation that comes from no one understanding the struggle is difficult, not easy. The lack of support from people who do not understand the nature of the disability, the judgment, the fear, is not easy. The more the faith community can bridge these gaps in a lovingly and compassionately, the more the isolation, loneliness, and anxiety can be lifted off of families. There are many resources and supports in the world for parents of children with autism, and that is a good thing, but why should a family have to seek out support from the world when they should be able to get it in their church community? The world is then where they find the support and acceptance that they are craving both for their child as well as for themselves in concerning this part of their life, as often the church cannot meet this need. However, where the parent and child may receive acceptance and understanding in terms of the disability in these worldly support groups, they often lack support in those groups in terms of their faith, making it yet another place where these two essential parts of their lives cannot converge.

When there is such a bifurcation, then families find themselves split in terms of supporting their child. They seek outside support in the world, which comes in the way of medical professionals, educators, and community agencies who all are trained to support individuals with autism in the practical pieces of the needs I spoke about above- communication/social skills, adaptive skills (daily living skills), fine and gross motor skills, and specialized academic instruction to meet the student's educational needs. Through these support systems, families are given the practical tools they need and have to work on implementing these useful tools in their homes, schools, and communities. Then they go to church, where nothing related to their practical life is mentioned or taught or even accommodated within the setting. There are no specific prayers that they can apply to those practical things that they are implementing at home. However, we know that the most powerful support we can use in any situation is when faith and works are combined with a specific need.

The other area in which the faith community can provide powerful support is in supporting the uniqueness of each child with autism, and the call that God has on their life. In the medical and educational fields, where most families get all of their practical support from, there is often a deficit model used, where all of the weaknesses and deficits of the child are the areas of focus and intervention. From a practical standpoint, this makes sense. Nevertheless, from a human/parent perspective, this is probably the area that hurts the most (and references back to the grieving process mentioned earlier). What gets lost during therapy and specialized supports for the child is the child's individuality, their personality, their strengths, their beauty. What can make a parent feel the most despairing at times are the deficits that are always focused on, which can sometimes feel insurmountable. The faith community has the unique opportunity to come alongside these parents and children and speak life into these children, and speak purpose and destiny into these children, in a way that highlights the unique characteristics that were given to them by God for a specific purpose. This is something the medical and educational fields can never do but is something crucial for restoring hope and for providing the peace that comes with knowing that there is a purpose for the life that was given to the child, despite the disability. This view of the child can change the perspective from the deficit model described previously to a strengths-based model instead.

This is where Karla's book, #jeremiahspeaks, fills such an essential need and such a large gap, which is why I am so excited for this resource for families and churches as well. My prayer is that this begins a new chapter of convergence between the faith community and the disability community, where the families affected are embraced and loved within their church communities, and provision made for their children to be a part of the community is provided, and where practical resources and tools can also be shared.

Radha Richmond, M.A., Ed.S, is a Licensed Educational Psychologist (CA LEP #3249) who has spent more than a decade working with children with autism and their families in the educational setting.

Sarah Morgan

"Then said I, Ah, Lord GOD! behold, I cannot speak: for I am a child. Say not..." Jeremiah 1:6-7

Speech is the faculty or act of speaking. It is the faculty or act of expressing or describing thoughts, feelings, or perceptions by the articulation of words. Speech is what is spoken or expressed, as in conversation, to make known one's desires and intentions.

Everything God created was through the medium of speech. When God spoke in the beginning, He didn't speak to communicate, He spoke to create and bring into manifestation the world He wanted. Hebrews 11:3, *"By faith we understand the ages to have been prepared by a saying of God, [He Spoke] in regard to the things seen not having come out of things appearing;"* (Emphasis Added)! He created with the mind and articulated with words through speech and it was so. All through Genesis chapter one we see the creative process by the words **"And God Said" "And God Saw"**.

Subsequently, the inability to speak or the speech impediment in a person's life though medically diagnosed and deemed as a condition, carries deep spiritual roots orchestrated by the enemy(our adversary) the devil to undermine man's greatest likeness to his creator, which is the power of speech which enables him to express or describe his thoughts, feelings, or perceptions by the articulation of words and hence create the world and environment he desires.

Jesus dealt with this condition probably not called Autism in His day, but rather as one that had a deaf and dumb spirit. First, we must understand that it is a spirit, which means the condition is spiritual.

> *"One in the crowd answered, "**Teacher, I brought You my son, who has a mute spirit.** Wherever it takes hold on him, it dashes him to the ground. And he foams at the mouth and gnashes with his teeth and becomes rigid. And I told Your disciples so that they would cast it out, but they could not."* [Mark 9:17-18]

Secondly, the spirit was named. He called it a Dumb and Deaf spirit, and He rebuked it.

> *"When Jesus saw that the people came running together, He rebuked the foul spirit, saying unto him, '**Thou Dumb and Deaf spirit,** I charge thee, come out of him, and enter no more into him'. And the spirit cried, and rent him sore, and come out of him..."* [Mark 9:25, 26]

The miracle of the man who was deaf and had an

impediment in his speech is narrated by Mark 7:32-37 as follows:

> "And they bring unto Him one that was deaf and had an impediment in his speech, and they beseech him to lay his hand upon him. And He took him aside from the multitude privately, and put his fingers into his ears, and he spat and touched his tongue; and looking up to heaven, He sighed, and saith unto him Ephphatha , that is, Be opened. And his ears were opened, and **the bond of his tongue was loosed,** and **he spake plain,** And he charged them that they should tell no man ; but the more he charged them, so much the more a great deal they published it. And they were beyond measure astonished, saying, He hath done all things well ; **He maketh even the deaf to hear, and the dumb to speak."**

This miracle of recovery of speech and hearing was as a result of the prayer declaration that Jesus made directly to the dumb and deaf spirits.

In this book, #jeremiahspeaks, Karla has clearly, simply, and scripturally laid out 40 days of prayer declarations for a 40 day challenge specifically addressing this spiritual impediment (medically known as Autism) by having faith and confidence in God and His Word, knowing that He hears and answers prayer, that you too may say to that loved one "**Say not that you cannot Speak".**

> "Then the LORD asked Moses, "Who makes a person's mouth? Who decides whether people speak or do not speak, hear or do not hear, see or do not see? Is it not I, the LORD? Exodus 4:11

If you have selected this book, #jeremiahspeaks get ready to experience the miracle of **Speech** for your loved ones as you, by faith, open your mouth and pray these declarations by faith.

I am witness to the healing power of God, and yes God does Heal Autism. We will forever give Him Glory because He deserves it.

Thank you, Karla, for this addition of hope to the many who are fighting this battle. With God and Prayer, we Win!

Sarah Morgan
Prayer Academy Ministries, Inc.
Los Angeles, CA

ACKNOWLEDGMENTS

I will never fail to acknowledge my Grandparents, Peter and Mary Williams; my parents, Charles Allen and Annie Lee Turner. I am who I am because you laid a solid foundation of prayer in my life. I honor you.

A special thank you to *Sarah Morgan*. Your encouragement, contribution, and prayers for this project assisted me over the finished line. I give thanks to God, the Father, Jesus Christ, the *Son of the Living God*, and Holy Spirit for you being in life in this season. May the God who hears and answers prayers, never fail to hear and answer you!

Radha, you were God's choice. Words cannot express how thankful I am for your insight. It's time to write your book!

Jill Adams, Kimberly Allen, Christian Nickolas, and the rest of my family, Tim and Dasha Moore; and Rufus and Jamila Chambers, thank you for being an inspiration, consistent encouragement, and always challenging me to be the best version of myself.

Jackie Seeno, Debra Porter, and Ramanda Clarke, a three-fold cord is not easily broken. We have four! Thank you for your love and prayers.

Finally, thank you to each family member, friend, and intercessor, who in some way, contributed. You are appreciated.

INTRODUCTION

"Dear friends, do you think you'll get anywhere in this if you learn all the right words but never do anything? Does merely talking about faith indicate that a person really has it? For instance, you come upon an old friend dressed in rags and half-starved and say, "Good morning, friend! Be clothed in Christ! Be filled with the Holy Spirit!" and walk off without providing so much as a coat or a cup of soup—where does that get you? Isn't it obvious that God-talk without God-acts is outrageous nonsense?

I can already hear one of you agreeing by saying, "Sounds good. You take care of the faith department, I'll handle the works department."

Not so fast. You can no more show me your works apart from your faith than I can show you my faith apart from my works. Faith and works, works and faith, fit together hand in glove" (James 2:14-18 MSG).

This book is designed to encourage you to combine prayer, along with practical resources for the well-being and wholeness of your loved ones. As Autism Spectrum Disorder (ASD) continues to rise at a shocking rate, it is time for the faith-based community to stand between God and a generation of voiceless children. #jeremiahspeaks is designed to assist you to believe, "Jesus Christ the same yesterday, and today, and forever." —Hebrews 13:8. Jesus still opens blind eyes, deaf ears, and causes the nonverbal to SPEAK! In

#jeremiahspeaks, you will learn:

- To pray scriptural prayers for those diagnosed with ASD, especially those who are non-verbal.
- Increase your ability to pray faith-filled scripturally-based prayers.
- The power of the prayer of agreement.
- To fast and pray for your miracle breakthrough.
- To become aware of the practical resources that are available to you.

Preparing for the Journey

The following scriptures and confessions will assist you and your family to prepare as you begin to pray, confess the Word of God, and fast for the well-being of your loved ones. I encourage you, also, as part of your preparation to take the time to fill in the name (s) of those you are praying for and to let your daily confession and #hashtag be #_____**speaks!**

"Then Joshua told the people, "Purify yourselves, for tomorrow the LORD *will do great wonders among you"* (Joshua 1:5).

Scripture Meditation

Gal 3:13-14: *Christ hath redeemed us from the curse of the law, being made a curse for us: for it is written, Cursed is every one that hangeth on a tree: That the blessing of Abraham might come on the Gentiles through Jesus Christ; that we might receive the promise of the Spirit through faith.*

Col 2:14-15: *Blotting out the handwriting of ordinances that was against us, which was contrary to us, and took it out of the way, nailing it to his cross; And having spoiled principalities and powers, he made a shew of them openly, triumphing over them in it.*

Confessions

- Father, we ask as a family that You reveal to us any known or unknown curse(s) that may be at work in our family bloodline on both sides of our family. (Whatever the Lord reveals to you, declare that it is broken)
- We thank You for the release that You secured for us when You became a curse on the cross.
- We ask You to forgive our ancestors and us for any sin that has exposed us to a curse (name any specific sin that you are aware of or that the Holy Spirit Reveals). We receive Your forgiveness, and we choose to forgive those who have sinned against us (name each person by name).
- I break any ungodly ties that still bind me to anyone in my life who has ever hurt or disappointed me or to whom I have related to sinfully. (Name these people as you break the unhealthy bonds and soul ties.)
- I renounce all contact with the occult and promise to destroy all occult objects that I may possess. (Name the specific occult involvement.)
- I renounce all sexual sins, and I break the power of pornography that may have a hold on me.
- I renounce all self-inflicted curses that I have pronounced on myself, and I break those patterns from my heart and tongue.
- I renounce all curses that I have spoken against others, whether knowingly or unknowingly: gossip, bitter words, anger, and judgment. I break the authority of any such occult power in my life.
- I renounce all unholy covenants in which my ancestors or I have been involved (name them).
- I renounce all patterns of stinginess with finances that my ancestors or I have engaged. I resolve to be obedient to the Lord in the area of tithes and offerings.
- I renounce all attitudes of reliance upon man and the

flesh. I choose to place my trust in the Lord Jesus Christ.

- I do once and for all release myself from the power and authorities of any curse.
- All demonic spirits and powers involved (name them if they've been discerned), I bind you and command you to cease your activity in my life and to leave my life, my body, my soul, my mind, my family, my house, my job, etc.
- I pray all these things in the authority of the name of Jesus. Father, I give You thanks and praise you have heard and answered.

DAY 1

SCRIPTURE MEDITATION

1. *For whatsoever is born of God overcometh the world: and this is the victory that overcometh the world, [even] our faith.* [1Jo 5:4 KJV]

2. *And they overcame him by the blood of the Lamb, and by the word of their testimony; and they loved not their lives unto the death.* [Rev 12:11 KJV]

3. And through him to reconcile to himself all things, whether things on earth or things in heaven, by making peace through his blood, shed on the cross. [Colossians 1:20]

CONFESSIONS

- We release the blood of Jesus into _____ brain to destroy strongholds, arguments, reasoning's and thoughts that war against your truth, your Word and the knowledge of God, for _____ destiny, life; social, emotional, psychological, physiological, physical, and academic development, in Jesus' name.

- We decree and declare that ALL things pertaining to _____ destiny, life, social and educational development re reconciled by the blood of Jesus

- We decree _____ is redeemed by the Blood of the Lamb out of the hand of the enemy, in Jesus' name. Thank you, Lord Jesus Christ, for the Blood You shed and that Your blood FOREVER SPEAKS on _____ behalf.

- Father, we thank you that _____ and our family have overcome by the Blood of the Lamb and the word of our testimony, in Jesus' name.

- We invoke the power of the far superior blood of Jesus Christ over _____ and our family.
- It was for freedom that You shed Your blood; therefore, we declare _____ is free to speak because of the blood of Jesus Christ.
- We decree and declare because of the blood of Jesus _____ is delivered.
- We declare that the power in the blood is speaking and mediating on behalf of _____ and our family.
- We declare that _____, and our family's lives are soaked in the Blood of Jesus, and they are protected, and every ungodly cycle is broken.
- We apply the Blood of Jesus over our lives for peace, in Jesus' name. WE AGREE!

#_____**speaks**

DAY 2

SCRIPTURE MEDITATION

1. *The Spirit of the LORD spake by me, and his word [was] in my tongue. [2Sa 23:2 KJV]*

2. *Grace and peace be multiplied unto you through the knowledge of God, and of Jesus our Lord, [2Pe 1:2 KJV]*

3. *I ask—ask the God of our Master, Jesus Christ, the God of glory—to make you intelligent and discerning in knowing him personally, your eyes focused and clear, so that you can see exactly what it is he is calling you to do, grasp the immensity of this glorious way of life he has for his followers, oh, the utter extravagance of his work in us who trust him—endless energy, boundless strength! [Ephesians 1:17-19 MSG]*

CONFESSIONS

- Father, You are the God of miracles, as a family, we agree with your that the Word is in _____ Tongue, and you will speak through _____ _____in Jesus' name.

- We declare grace and peace are multiplied to (insert the names of the parents, caregivers, medical professionals, educators, and community agencies) __

  _____
  _____
  _____
  _____working with _____
  _____through the knowledge of God, and of Jesus our Lord, in Jesus' name. WE AGREE!

- May God grant (insert the names of the parents, caregivers, medical professionals, educators, and

community agencies) _____
_____
_____
_____
working with_____divine insight, wisdom, and intelligence, endless energy, and boundless strength.

- Open the eyes of our family members who do not know you so that they turn from darkness to light and from the power of satan to God, that they may receive forgiveness of sins and a place among those who are sanctified by faith in You.' (Acts 26:18), in Jesus' name.

#_____**speaks**

DAY 3

SCRIPTURE MEDITATION

1. *And my tongue shall speak of thy righteousness [and] of thy praise all the day long. [Psa 35:28 KJV]*

2. *Grace and peace be multiplied unto you through the knowledge of God, and of Jesus our Lord, [2Pe 1:2 KJV]*

3. *I ask—ask the God of our Master, Jesus Christ, the God of glory—to make you intelligent and discerning in knowing him personally, your eyes focused and clear, so that you can see exactly what it is he is calling you to do, grasp the immensity of this glorious way of life he has for his followers, oh, the utter extravagance of his work in us who trust him—endless energy, boundless strength! [Ephesians 1:17-19 MSG]*

CONFESSIONS

- Father, we declare that _____ tongue speaks your righteousness and of your praise all day long, in Jesus' name.

- We declare grace and peace are multiplied to (insert the names of the parents, caregivers, medical professionals, educators, and community agencies) __

  _____
  _____
  _____
  _____ working with _____
  _____ through the knowledge of God, and of Jesus our Lord, in Jesus' name. WE AGREE!

- May God grant (insert the names of the parents, caregivers, medical professionals, educators, and community agencies) _____

_____

_____
_____
_____
working with_____divine insight, wisdom, and intelligence, endless energy, and boundless strength.

- Open the eyes of our family members who do not know you so that they turn from darkness to light and from the power of satan to God, that they may receive forgiveness of sins and a place among those who are sanctified by faith in You.' (Acts 26:18), in Jesus' name.

#_____speaks

DAY 4

SCRIPTURE MEDITATION

1. *[[To the chief Musician upon Shoshannim, for the sons of Korah, Maschil, A Song of loves.]] My heart is inditing a good matter: I speak of the things which I have made touching the king: my tongue [is] the pen of a ready writer. [Psa 45:1 KJV]*

2. *Grace and peace be multiplied unto you through the knowledge of God, and of Jesus our Lord, [2Pe 1:2 KJV]*

3. *I ask—ask the God of our Master, Jesus Christ, the God of glory—to make you intelligent and discerning in knowing him personally, your eyes focused and clear, so that you can see exactly what it is he is calling you to do, grasp the immensity of this glorious way of life he has for his followers, oh, the utter extravagance of his work in us who trust him—endless energy, boundless strength! [Ephesians 1:17-19 MSG]*

CONFESSIONS

- Father, we declare that _____tongue is the pen of a ready writer, in Jesus' name.

- We declare grace and peace are multiplied to (insert the names of the parents, caregivers, medical professionals, educators, and community agencies) __
_____
_____
_____
_____working with _____
_____through the knowledge of God, and of Jesus our Lord, in Jesus' name. WE AGREE!

- May God grant (insert the names of the parents,

caregivers, medical professionals, educators, and community agencies) _____
_____
_____
_____
working with_____ divine insight, wisdom, and intelligence, endless energy, and boundless strength.

- Open the eyes of our family members who do not know you so that they turn from darkness to light and from the power of satan to God, that they may receive forgiveness of sins and a place among those who are sanctified by faith in You.' (Acts 26:18), in Jesus' name.

#_____**speaks**

DAY 5

SCRIPTURE MEDITATION

1. *Deliver me from blood guiltiness, O God, thou God of my salvation: [and] my tongue shall sing aloud of thy righteousness. [Psalm 51:14 KJV] 14*

2. *Grace and peace be multiplied unto you through the knowledge of God, and of Jesus our Lord, [2Pe 1:2 KJV]*

3. *I ask—ask the God of our Master, Jesus Christ, the God of glory—to make you intelligent and discerning in knowing him personally, your eyes focused and clear, so that you can see exactly what it is he is calling you to do, grasp the immensity of this glorious way of life he has for his followers, oh, the utter extravagance of his work in us who trust him—endless energy, boundless strength! [Ephesians 1:17-19 MSG]*

CONFESSIONS

- Father, we declare that _____ tongue sings aloud of your righteousness, in Jesus' name.

- We declare grace and peace are multiplied to (insert the names of the parents, caregivers, medical professionals, educators, and community agencies) __

    _____
    _____
    _____
    _____ working with _____
    _____ through the knowledge of God, and of Jesus our Lord, in Jesus' name. WE AGREE!

- May God grant (insert the names of the parents, caregivers, medical professionals, educators, and community agencies) _____

_____

_____
_____
_____

working with_____divine insight, wisdom, and intelligence, endless energy, and boundless strength.

- Open the eyes of our family members who do not know you so that they turn from darkness to light and from the power of satan to God, that they may receive forgiveness of sins and a place among those who are sanctified by faith in You.' (Acts 26:18), in Jesus' name.

#_____**speaks**

DAY 6

SCRIPTURE MEDITATION

1. *My tongue also shall talk of thy righteousness all the day long: for they are confounded, for they are brought unto shame, that seek my hurt. [Psalms 71:24 KJV]*

2. *Grace and peace be multiplied unto you through the knowledge of God, and of Jesus our Lord, [2Pe 1:2 KJV]*

3. *I ask—ask the God of our Master, Jesus Christ, the God of glory—to make you intelligent and discerning in knowing him personally, your eyes focused and clear, so that you can see exactly what it is he is calling you to do, grasp the immensity of this glorious way of life he has for his followers, oh, the utter extravagance of his work in us who trust him—endless energy, boundless strength! [Ephesians 1:17-19 MSG]*

CONFESSIONS

- Father, we declare that _____ tongue will speak of your righteousness all day long, in Jesus' name.

- We declare grace and peace are multiplied to (insert the names of the parents, caregivers, medical professionals, educators, and community agencies) __
_____
_____
_____
_____ working with _____
_____ through the knowledge of God, and of Jesus our Lord, in Jesus' name. WE AGREE!

- May God grant (insert the names of the parents,

caregivers, medical professionals, educators, and community agencies) _____
_____
_____
_____
working with_____divine insight, wisdom, and intelligence, endless energy, and boundless strength.

- Open the eyes of our family members who do not know you so that they turn from darkness to light and from the power of satan to God, that they may receive forgiveness of sins and a place among those who are sanctified by faith in You.' (Acts 26:18), in Jesus' name.

#_____**speaks**

DAY 7

Scripture Meditation

1. *My tongue shall speak of thy word: for all thy commandments [are] righteousness. [Psalms 119:172 KJV]*

2. *Grace and peace be multiplied unto you through the knowledge of God, and of Jesus our Lord, [2Pe 1:2 KJV]*

3. *I ask—ask the God of our Master, Jesus Christ, the God of glory—to make you intelligent and discerning in knowing him personally, your eyes focused and clear, so that you can see exactly what it is he is calling you to do, grasp the immensity of this glorious way of life he has for his followers, oh, the utter extravagance of his work in us who trust him—endless energy, boundless strength! [Ephesians 1:17-19 MSG]*

Confessions

- Father, we declare _____ tongue speaks of your Word.

- We declare grace and peace are multiplied to (insert the names of the parents, caregivers, medical professionals, educators, and community agencies) __
_____
_____
_____
_____ working with _____
_____ through the knowledge of God, and of Jesus our Lord, in Jesus' name. WE AGREE!

- May God grant (insert the names of the parents, caregivers, medical professionals, educators, and community agencies) _____

_____
_____
_____

working with_____divine insight, wisdom, and intelligence, endless energy, and boundless strength.

- Open the eyes of our family members who do not know you so that they turn from darkness to light and from the power of satan to God, that they may receive forgiveness of sins and a place among those who are sanctified by faith in You.' (Acts 26:18), in Jesus' name.

   #_____**speaks**

DAY 8

Scripture Meditation

1. *[[A Song of degrees.]] When the LORD turned again the captivity of Zion, we were like them that dream. 2 Then was our mouth filled with laughter, and our tongue with singing: then said they among the heathen, The LORD hath done great things for them. 3 The LORD hath done great things for us; [whereof] we are glad. [Psalms 126:1-3 KJV]*

2. *Grace and peace be multiplied unto you through the knowledge of God, and of Jesus our Lord, [2Pe 1:2 KJV]*

3. *I ask—ask the God of our Master, Jesus Christ, the God of glory—to make you intelligent and discerning in knowing him personally, your eyes focused and clear, so that you can see exactly what it is he is calling you to do, grasp the immensity of this glorious way of life he has for his followers, oh, the utter extravagance of his work in us who trust him—endless energy, boundless strength! [Ephesians 1:17-19 MSG]*

Confessions

- Father, we declare _____ tongue is filled with laughter and with singing.

- We declare grace and peace are multiplied to (insert the names of the parents, caregivers, medical professionals, educators, and community agencies) __

   _____
   _____
   _____
   _____ working with _____
   _____ through the knowledge of God, and of Jesus our Lord, in Jesus' name. WE AGREE!

- May God grant (insert the names of the parents, caregivers, medical professionals, educators, and community agencies) _____
_____
_____
_____
working with_____divine insight, wisdom, and intelligence, endless energy, and boundless strength.
- Open the eyes of our family members who do not know you so that they turn from darkness to light and from the power of satan to God, that they may receive forgiveness of sins and a place among those who are sanctified by faith in You.' (Acts 26:18), in Jesus' name.

#_____**speaks**

DAY 9

SCRIPTURE MEDITATION

1. *Turn again our captivity, O LORD, as the streams in the south. 5 They that sow in tears shall reap in joy. 6 He that goeth forth and weepeth, bearing precious seed, shall doubtless come again with rejoicing, bringing his sheaves [with him]. [Psa 126:4-6 KJV]*

2. *Grace and peace be multiplied unto you through the knowledge of God, and of Jesus our Lord, [2Pe 1:2 KJV]*

3. *I ask—ask the God of our Master, Jesus Christ, the God of glory—to make you intelligent and discerning in knowing him personally, your eyes focused and clear, so that you can see exactly what it is he is calling you to do, grasp the immensity of this glorious way of life he has for his followers, oh, the utter extravagance of his work in us who trust him—endless energy, boundless strength! [Ephesians 1:17-19 MSG]*

CONFESSIONS

- Father, we thank you that _____ rejoices and reaps in joy for every frustrating tear and receives the restoration of all things concerning his life, in Jesus' name.

- We declare grace and peace are multiplied to (insert the names of the parents, caregivers, medical professionals, educators, and community agencies) __
_____
_____
_____
_____ working with _____
_____ through the knowledge of God, and of Jesus our Lord, in Jesus' name. WE AGREE!

- May God grant (insert the names of the parents, caregivers, medical professionals, educators, and community agencies) _____
  _____
  _____
  working with_____divine insight, wisdom, and intelligence, endless energy, and boundless strength.
- Open the eyes of our family members who do not know you so that they turn from darkness to light and from the power of satan to God, that they may receive forgiveness of sins and a place among those who are sanctified by faith in You.' (Acts 26:18), in Jesus' name.

#_____**speaks**

DAY 10

Scripture Meditation

1. *The tongue of the just [is as] choice silver: the heart of the wicked [is] little worth. [Pro 10:20 KJV]*

2. *Grace and peace be multiplied unto you through the knowledge of God, and of Jesus our Lord, [2Pe 1:2 KJV]*

3. *I ask—ask the God of our Master, Jesus Christ, the God of glory—to make you intelligent and discerning in knowing him personally, your eyes focused and clear, so that you can see exactly what it is he is calling you to do, grasp the immensity of this glorious way of life he has for his followers, oh, the utter extravagance of his work in us who trust him—endless energy, boundless strength! [Ephesians 1:17-19 MSG]*

Confessions

- Father, we declare _____ tongue is as choice silver, in Jesus' name.

- We declare grace and peace are multiplied to (insert the names of the parents, caregivers, medical professionals, educators, and community agencies) __
  _____
  _____
  _____
  _____ working with _____
  _____ through the knowledge of God, and of Jesus our Lord, in Jesus' name. WE AGREE!

- May God grant (insert the names of the parents, caregivers, medical professionals, educators, and community agencies) _____
  _____

_____
_____
working with_____divine insight, wisdom, and intelligence, endless energy, and boundless strength.

- Open the eyes of our family members who do not know you so that they turn from darkness to light and from the power of satan to God, that they may receive forgiveness of sins and a place among those who are sanctified by faith in You.' (Acts 26:18), in Jesus' name.

    #_____**speaks**

DAY 11

Scripture Meditation

1. *There is that speaketh like the piercings of a sword: but the tongue of the wise [is] health. [Pro 12:18 KJV]*

2. *Grace and peace be multiplied unto you through the knowledge of God, and of Jesus our Lord, [2Pe 1:2 KJV]*

3. *I ask—ask the God of our Master, Jesus Christ, the God of glory—to make you intelligent and discerning in knowing him personally, your eyes focused and clear, so that you can see exactly what it is he is calling you to do, grasp the immensity of this glorious way of life he has for his followers, oh, the utter extravagance of his work in us who trust him—endless energy, boundless strength! [Ephesians 1:17-19 MSG]*

Confessions

- Father, we declare _____ tongue is the tongue of the wise and produces health, in the name of Jesus.

- We declare grace and peace are multiplied to (insert the names of the parents, caregivers, medical professionals, educators, and community agencies) __
  _____
  _____
  _____
  _____ working with _____
  _____ through the knowledge of God, and of Jesus our Lord, in Jesus' name. WE AGREE!

- May God grant (insert the names of the parents, caregivers, medical professionals, educators, and community agencies) _____

_____
_____
_____

working with_____divine insight, wisdom, and intelligence, endless energy, and boundless strength.

- Open the eyes of our family members who do not know you so that they turn from darkness to light and from the power of satan to God, that they may receive forgiveness of sins and a place among those who are sanctified by faith in You.' (Acts 26:18), in Jesus' name.

#_____**speaks**

DAY 12

SCRIPTURE MEDITATION

1. *A wholesome tongue [is] a tree of life: but perverseness therein [is] a breach in the spirit. [Pro 15:4 KJV]*
2. *Grace and peace are multiplied unto you through the knowledge of God, and of Jesus our Lord, [2Pe 1:2 KJV]*
3. *I ask—ask the God of our Master, Jesus Christ, the God of glory—to make you intelligent and discerning in knowing him personally, your eyes focused and clear, so that you can see exactly what it is he is calling you to do, grasp the immensity of this glorious way of life he has for his followers, oh, the utter extravagance of his work in us who trust him—endless energy, boundless strength! [Ephesians 1:17-19 MSG]*

CONFESSIONS

- Father, we declare _____ tongue is a tree of life, in Jesus' name.
- We declare grace and peace are multiplied to (insert the names of the parents, caregivers, medical professionals, educators, and community agencies) __
  _____
  _____
  _____
  _____ working with _____
  _____ through the knowledge of God, and of Jesus our Lord, in Jesus' name. WE AGREE!
- May God grant (insert the names of the parents, caregivers, medical professionals, educators, and community agencies) _____

_____
_____
_____

working with _____ divine insight, wisdom, and intelligence, endless energy, and boundless strength.

- Open the eyes of our family members who do not know you so that they turn from darkness to light and from the power of satan to God, that they may receive forgiveness of sins and a place among those who are sanctified by faith in You.' (Acts 26:18), in Jesus' name.

#_____speaks

DAY 13

Scripture Meditation

1. *The preparations of the heart in man, and the answer of the tongue, [is] from the LORD. [Pro 16:1 KJV]*

2. *Grace and peace be multiplied unto you through the knowledge of God, and of Jesus our Lord, [2Pe 1:2 KJV]*

3. *I ask—ask the God of our Master, Jesus Christ, the God of glory—to make you intelligent and discerning in knowing him personally, your eyes focused and clear, so that you can see exactly what it is he is calling you to do, grasp the immensity of this glorious way of life he has for his followers, oh, the utter extravagance of his work in us who trust him—endless energy, boundless strength! [Ephesians 1:17-19 MSG]*

Confessions

- We declare all of _____ answers are from the Lord Jesus Christ, and his tongue speaks forth those answers with the power and might of God, in Jesus' name.

- We declare grace and peace are multiplied to (insert the names of the parents, caregivers, medical professionals, educators, and community agencies) __
_____
_____
_____
_____ working with _____
_____ through the knowledge of God, and of Jesus our Lord, in Jesus' name. WE AGREE!

- May God grant (insert the names of the parents, caregivers, medical professionals, educators, and

community agencies) _____
_____
_____

working with_____divine insight, wisdom, and intelligence, endless energy, and boundless strength.

- Open the eyes of our family members who do not know you so that they turn from darkness to light and from the power of satan to God, that they may receive forgiveness of sins and a place among those who are sanctified by faith in You.' (Acts 26:18), in Jesus' name.

#_____**speaks**

DAY 14

Scripture Meditation

1. *Death and life [are] in the power of the tongue: and they that love it shall eat the fruit thereof. [Pro 18:21 KJV]*

2. *Grace and peace be multiplied unto you through the knowledge of God, and of Jesus our Lord, [2Pe 1:2 KJV]*

3. *I ask—ask the God of our Master, Jesus Christ, the God of glory—to make you intelligent and discerning in knowing him personally, your eyes focused and clear, so that you can see exactly what it is he is calling you to do, grasp the immensity of this glorious way of life he has for his followers, oh, the utter extravagance of his work in us who trust him—endless energy, boundless strength! [Ephesians 1:17-19 MSG]*

Confessions

- Father, we declare we eat of the fruit of _____ _____ tongue, in Jesus' name.

- We declare grace and peace are multiplied to (insert the names of the parents, caregivers, medical professionals, educators, and community agencies) __
_____
_____
_____
_____ working with _____
_____ through the knowledge of God, and of Jesus our Lord, in Jesus' name. WE AGREE!

- May God grant (insert the names of the parents, caregivers, medical professionals, educators, and

community agencies) _____
_____
_____
working with_____divine insight, wisdom, and intelligence, endless energy, and boundless strength.

- Open the eyes of our family members who do not know you so that they turn from darkness to light and from the power of satan to God, that they may receive forgiveness of sins and a place among those who are sanctified by faith in You.' (Acts 26:18), in Jesus' name.

#_____**speaks**

DAY 15

Scripture Meditation

1. *Strengthen ye the weak hands, and confirm the feeble knees. Say to them [that are] of a fearful heart, Be strong, fear not: behold, your God will come [with] vengeance, [even] God [with] a recompense; he will come and save you. Then the eyes of the blind shall be opened, and the ears of the deaf shall be unstopped. Then shall the lame [man] leap as an hart, and the tongue of the dumb sing: for in the wilderness shall waters break out, and streams in the desert. [Isa 35:3-6 KJV]*

2. *Grace and peace be multiplied unto you through the knowledge of God, and of Jesus our Lord, [2Pe 1:2 KJV]*

3. *I ask—ask the God of our Master, Jesus Christ, the God of glory—to make you intelligent and discerning in knowing him personally, your eyes focused and clear, so that you can see exactly what it is he is calling you to do, grasp the immensity of this glorious way of life he has for his followers, oh, the utter extravagance of his work in us who trust him—endless energy, boundless strength! [Ephesians 1:17-19 MSG]*

Confessions

- Father, we declare as you visit _____ you come with vengeance and recompense so that his tongue sings and flows like streams of water in the desert, in the name of Jesus.
- We declare grace and peace are multiplied to (insert the names of the parents, caregivers, medical professionals, educators, and community agencies) __

_____
_____
_____working with _____
_____through the knowledge of God, and of Jesus our Lord, in Jesus' name. WE AGREE!

- May God grant (insert the names of the parents, caregivers, medical professionals, educators, and community agencies) _____
_____
_____
_____
working with_____divine insight, wisdom, and intelligence, endless energy, and boundless strength.

- Open the eyes of our family members who do not know you so that they turn from darkness to light and from the power of satan to God, that they may receive forgiveness of sins and a place among those who are sanctified by faith in You.' (Acts 26:18), in Jesus' name.

#_____**speaks**

DAY 16

SCRIPTURE MEDITATION

1. *The Lord GOD hath given me the tongue of the learned, that I should know how to speak a word in season to [him that is] weary: he wakeneth morning by morning, he wakeneth mine ear to hear as the learned. [Isa 50:4 KJV]*

2. *Grace and peace be multiplied unto you through the knowledge of God, and of Jesus our Lord, [2Pe 1:2 KJV]*

3. *I ask—ask the God of our Master, Jesus Christ, the God of glory—to make you intelligent and discerning in knowing him personally, your eyes focused and clear, so that you can see exactly what it is he is calling you to do, grasp the immensity of this glorious way of life he has for his followers, oh, the utter extravagance of his work in us who trust him—endless energy, boundless strength! [Ephesians 1:17-19 MSG]*

CONFESSIONS

- Father, we declare _____ has the tongue of the learned, and that he knows how to speak a word in season because he knows your voice.

- We declare grace and peace are multiplied to (insert the names of the parents, caregivers, medical professionals, educators, and community agencies) __

  _____
  _____
  _____
  _____ working with _____
  _____ through the knowledge of God, and of Jesus our Lord, in Jesus' name. WE AGREE!

- May God grant (insert the names of the parents, caregivers, medical professionals, educators, and community agencies) _____
  _____
  _____
  _____
  working with _____ divine insight, wisdom, and intelligence, endless energy, and boundless strength.
- Open the eyes of our family members who do not know you so that they turn from darkness to light and from the power of satan to God, that they may receive forgiveness of sins and a place among those who are sanctified by faith in You.' (Acts 26:18), in Jesus' name.

  #_____**speaks**

DAY 17

SCRIPTURE MEDITATION

1. *And they bring unto him one that was deaf, and had an impediment in his speech; and they beseech him to put his hand upon him. And he took him aside from the multitude, and put his fingers into his ears, and he spit, and touched his tongue; And looking up to heaven, he sighed, and saith unto him, Ephphatha, that is, Be opened. And straightway his ears were opened, and the string of his tongue was loosed, and he spake plain. And he charged them that they should tell no man: but the more he charged them, so much the more a great deal they published [it]; And were beyond measure astonished, saying, He hath done all things well: he maketh both the deaf to hear, and the dumb to speak. [Mar 7:32-37 KJV]*

2. *Grace and peace be multiplied unto you through the knowledge of God, and of Jesus our Lord, [2Pe 1:2 KJV]*

3. *I ask—ask the God of our Master, Jesus Christ, the God of glory—to make you intelligent and discerning in knowing him personally, your eyes focused and clear, so that you can see exactly what it is he is calling you to do, grasp the immensity of this glorious way of life he has for his followers, oh, the utter extravagance of his work in us who trust him—endless energy, boundless strength! [Ephesians 1:17-19 MSG]*

CONFESSIONS

- Father, you are not partial, but you are fair and just, therefore, as you did through Jesus when he was here on earth, touch _____ tongue and loose the string of his tongue that he may speak clearly, in Jesus' name.

- We declare grace and peace are multiplied to (insert the names of the parents, caregivers, medical professionals, educators, and community agencies) __

_____
_____
_____working with _____
_____through the knowledge of God, and of Jesus our Lord, in Jesus' name. WE AGREE!

- May God grant (insert the names of the parents, caregivers, medical professionals, educators, and community agencies) _____

_____
_____
_____working with_____divine insight, wisdom, and intelligence, endless energy, and boundless strength.

- Open the eyes of our family members who do not know you so that they turn from darkness to light and
- from the power of satan to God, that they may receive forgiveness of sins and a place among those who are sanctified by faith in You.' (Acts 26:18), in Jesus' name

#_____**speaks**

DAY 18

SCRIPTURE MEDITATION

- *And his mouth was opened immediately, and his tongue [loosed], and he spake, and praised God. [Luk 1:64 KJV]*
- *Grace and peace be multiplied unto you through the knowledge of God, and of Jesus our Lord, [2Pe 1:2 KJV]*
- *I ask—ask the God of our Master, Jesus Christ, the God of glory—to make you intelligent and discerning in knowing him personally, your eyes focused and clear, so that you can see exactly what it is he is calling you to do, grasp the immensity of this glorious way of life he has for his followers, oh, the utter extravagance of his work in us who trust him—endless energy, boundless strength! [Ephesians 1:17-19 MSG]*

CONFESSIONS

- Father, open _____ mouth and loose his tongue to speak and praise you, in Jesus' name.
- We declare grace and peace are multiplied to (insert the names of the parents, caregivers, medical professionals, educators, and community agencies) __

    _____
    _____
    _____
    _____ working with _____
    _____ through the knowledge of God, and of Jesus our Lord, in Jesus' name. WE AGREE!

- May God grant (insert the names of the parents, caregivers, medical professionals, educators, and

community agencies) _____
_____
_____
_____
working with_____ divine insight, wisdom, and intelligence, endless energy, and boundless strength.

- Open the eyes of our family members who do not know you so that they turn from darkness to light and from the power of satan to God, that they may receive forgiveness of sins and a place among those who are sanctified by faith in You.' (Acts 26:18), in Jesus' name.

#_____**speaks**

DAY 19

Now that we have asked God for _____'s miracle, we will commence to declare over _____ and ((Insert the name of parents) _____ destinies.

Scripture Meditation

1. *And now, Lord, behold their threatenings: and grant unto thy servants, that with all boldness they may speak thy word, By stretching forth thine hand to heal; and that signs and wonders may be done by the name of thy holy child Jesus. [Act 4:29-30 KJV]*

Confessions

- Lord, cause your Word to penetrate the depths of _____and bring all of his thought processes into alignment with your will, in Jesus' name.

- Every witchcraft power working against _____ and (Insert the name of parents) _____destinies be exposed and rendered helpless by the fire of God.

- Every incantation and ritual working against their destinies are condemned, in the name of Jesus.

- Every power of darkness assigned against their destinies, be exposed and rendered helpless by the fire of God.

- Every evil power trying to re-program their lives is already condemned, in the name of Jesus.

- Father, we declare, like David, _____ and (Insert the name of parents) _____ will fulfill God's plan for their lives, in their generations and speak of Your marvelous work in their lives, in

Jesus' name. WE AGREE!

#_____speaks

DAY 20

SCRIPTURE MEDITATION

1. *And his name through faith in his name hath made this man strong, whom ye see and know: yea, the faith which is by him hath given him this perfect soundness in the presence of you all. [Act 3:16 KJV]*

CONFESSIONS

- Lord, cause your voice to penetrate every part of ____ _____ piercing deep and penetrating deep into his bone marrow, rearranging the cell structures within his body, in Jesus' name.

- We reject every rearrangement of _____ and (Insert the name of parents)'s _____ destinies in the name of Jesus.

- Lord, anytime they want to make a mistake, correct their course.

- We declare they will not be removed from Your divine agenda, in the name of Jesus.

- We declare _____ and (Insert the name of parents) _____ are NOT limited by any power of darkness, in the name of Jesus.

- Father, we declare, like David, _____ and (Insert the name of parents) _____ will fulfill God's plan for their lives, in their generations and speak of Your marvelous work in their lives, in Jesus' name. WE AGREE!

#_____speaks

DAY 21

Scripture Meditation

1. *And God wrought special miracles by the hands of Paul: 12 So that from his body were brought unto the sick handkerchiefs or aprons, and the diseases departed from them, and the evil spirits went out of them. [Act 19:11-12 KJV]*

CONFESSIONS

- Lord, cause your blood and your Word to purify _____ _____ blood system, in Jesus' name.
- Every person, entity, organization, and evil influence working against the progress of _____ and (Insert the name of parents)'s _____ destinies will not prosper, in the name of Jesus.
- Lord, let their divine destinies be realized and let every altered destiny be nullified.
- We reject every satanic re-arrangement of their destinies, in the name of Jesus.
- We declare they will not live below their divine standard, in Jesus' name.
- Father, we declare, like David, _____ and (Insert the name of parents) _____ will fulfill God's plan for their lives, in their generations and speak of Your marvelous work in their lives, in Jesus' name. **WE AGREE!**

  #_____**speaks**

DAY 22

Scripture Meditation

1. *Long time therefore abode they speaking boldly in the Lord, which gave testimony unto the word of his grace, and granted signs and wonders to be done by their hands. [Act 14:3 KJV]*

Confessions

- We decree and declare that _____ speaks freely and fearlessly to bear testimony to the Word of His grace and of His signs and wonders.

- Lord, release the quickening power of Your blood into _____ to energize his/her blood and bone marrow with your perspective, in Jesus' name.

- Every evil power having a negative awareness of _____ _____ and (Insert the name of parents) ___ _____ destinies is impotent, in the name of Jesus.

- We paralyze everything and everyone with the intending to contaminate the destinies of _____ _____ and (Insert the name of parents)_____ _____, in the name of Jesus.

- Every damage done to _____ and (Insert the name of parents) _____ destinies is repaired and restored now, in the name of Jesus.

- Father, we declare, like David, _____ and (Insert the name of parents) _____ will fulfill God's plan for their lives, in their generations and speak of Your marvelous work in their lives, in

Jesus' name. WE AGREE

#_____speaks

DAY 23

SCRIPTURE MEDITATION

1. *And they went forth, and preached everywhere, the Lord working with [them], and confirming the word with signs following. Amen. [Mar 16:20 KJV]*

CONFESSIONS

- We release your blood into any trauma imprints and centers that have been lodged and erected in _____ _____memories, thought processes, and neural fibers. Lord, we ask you to cleanse (Insert name)'s mind, thought patterns, emotional patterns, and processes so that he/she may be pure and free to express the full identity you designed for him/her to express and demonstrate, in Jesus' name.

- Holy Spirit, we invite you to move and act upon _____ _____mind, in Jesus' name.

- Lord, restore _____ and (Insert the name of parents) _____ to Your original design for their lives.

- We reject destiny-demoting names and labels in the name of Jesus.

- Father, we declare, like David, _____ and (Insert the name of parents) _____ will fulfill God's plan for their lives, in their generations and speak of Your marvelous work in their lives, in Jesus' name. WE AGREE!

#_____speaks

DAY 24

SCRIPTURE MEDITATION

1. And these signs shall follow them that believe; In my name shall they cast out devils; they shall speak with new tongues; [Mar 16:17 KJV]

CONFESSIONS

- Lord, we ask for the anointing to see where disease is lodged in the body of _____ and those around us and we ask for the corresponding scripture and strategy to work creative miracles, healings and restoration through your power in us, in Jesus' name

- We declare that _____ and (Insert the name of parents) _____ will not operate below their divine destinies, in the name of Jesus.

- Lord, anoint their eyes, hand, legs, and feet to locate their divine purpose.

- Every power contending with their divine destiny, scatter by the hand of God, in the name of Jesus.

- Let the spirit of excellence come upon _____ and (Insert the name of parents_____, in Jesus' name.

- Father, we declare, like David, _____ and (Insert the name of parents) _____ will fulfill God's plan for their lives, in their generations and speak of Your marvelous work in their lives, in Jesus' name. WE AGREE!

#_____speaks

DAY 25

Scripture Meditation

1. *And God hath set some in the church, first apostles, secondarily prophets, thirdly teachers, after that miracles, then gifts of healings, helps, governments, diversities of tongues. [1Co 12:28 KJV]*

Confessions

- We submit _____ entire being to the Lord and ask you to conquer every enemy structure built within his mind and blood system, in Jesus' name.

- We resist and rebuke all efforts to change _____ _____ and (Insert the name of parents) _____ _____ destinies, in the name of Jesus.

- We remove from the enemy every right to rob _____ _____ and (Insert the name of parents) ___ _____ of their divine destinies, in the name of Jesus.

- We command all powers of darkness assigned to ____ _____ and (Insert the name of parents) ___ _____ destinies to leave and never return, in the name of Jesus.

- Father, we declare, like David, _____ and (Insert the name of parents) _____ will fulfill God's plan for their lives, in their generations and speak of Your marvelous work in their lives, in Jesus' name. **WE AGREE!**

#_____speaks

DAY 26

Scripture Meditation

1. *Therefore I make a decree, That every people, nation, and language, which speak anything amiss against the God of Shadrach, Meshach, and Abednego, shall be cut in pieces, and their houses shall be made a dunghill: because there is no other God that can deliver after this sort. [Dan 3:29 KJV]*

Confessions

- We decree the Spirit of Jesus is increasing continually in every part of _____, in Jesus' name!

- We command all the enemies of Jesus Christ that have access to, _____ and **(Insert the name of parents)** _____ progress to leave and never return, in the name of Jesus.

- We paralyze every satanic opportunity contending against their lives, in the name of Jesus.

- Every incantation, ritual and, witchcraft power working against their destinies, is nullified the power of the name and blood of Jesus.

- We render null and void the influence of destiny swallowers, downgrades, and thieves, in the name of Jesus.

- Father, we declare, like David, _____ and **(Insert the name of parents)** _____ will fulfill God's plan for their lives, in their generations and speak of Your marvelous work in their lives, in Jesus' name. WE AGREE!

#_____speaks

DAY 27

SCRIPTURE MEDITATION

1. *In the beginning, God created the heaven and the earth. 2 And the earth was without form, and void; and darkness [was] upon the face of the deep. And the Spirit of God moved upon the face of the waters. [Gen 1:1-2 KJV]*

CONFESSIONS

- We decree the DNA of Jesus Christ penetrates every cell of _____ body and that the DNA of Jesus Christ lives, rules, and reigns within him, in Jesus' name.

- We release the creative breath of God to blow upon (_____ for a creative miracle, in Jesus' name.

- Every household wickedness struggling to re-arrange _____ and **(Insert the name of parents)** ___ _____ destinies, loose your hold, in the name of Jesus.

- The rod of the wicked shall not rest upon their life, in the name of Jesus.

- We declare they will NOT be removed from the divine agenda of God, in the name of Jesus.

- Holy Spirit, we invite You into _____ and **(Insert the name of parents)** _____ imaginations.

- Father, we declare, like David, _____ and **(Insert the name of parents)** _____ will fulfill God's plan for their lives, in their generations and speak of Your marvelous work in their lives, in

Jesus' name. WE AGREE!

#_____speaks

DAY 28

Scripture Meditation

1. *Insomuch that they brought forth the sick into the streets, and laid [them] on beds and couches, that at the least the shadow of Peter passing by might overshadow some of them. There came also a multitude [out] of the cities round about unto Jerusalem, bringing sick folks, and them which were vexed with unclean spirits: and they were healed every one. [Act 5:15-16 KJV]*

Confessions

- We appropriate the work of the cross and Jesus' victory over death, hell, and the grave to all areas of _ _____life, in Jesus' name.

- Lord, bring to light every darkness shielding _____ _____ and **(Insert the name of parents)** _____ _____ potentials, in the name of Jesus.

- We break every curse of backwardness, in the name of Jesus.

- We recover _____ and **(Insert the name of parents)** _____ from every evil diversion, in Jesus' name.

- We declare that _____ and **(Insert the name of parents)** _____ have not come to the world in vain, in the name of Jesus.

- Father, we declare, like David, _____ and **(Insert the name of parents)** _____ will fulfill God's plan for their lives, in their generations and speak of Your marvelous work in their lives, in Jesus' name. WE AGREE!

#_____speaks

DAY 29

SCRIPTURE MEDITATION

2. *And Jesus said unto them, Because of your unbelief: for verily I say unto you, If ye have faith as a grain of mustard seed, ye shall say unto this mountain, Remove hence to yonder place; and it shall remove; and nothing shall be impossible unto you. Howbeit this kind goeth not out but by prayer and fasting. [Mat 17:20-21 KJV] 20*

CONFESSIONS

- We decree that _____ take on the DNA of Christ by being transformed progressively by the blood of Jesus flowing through his veins, arteries, and cells.

- We decree they are being transformed into the images and likeness of Christ by the Word of God and the Spirit of God bringing _____ into unity with the mind of Christ so he/she can do the Father's will, in Jesus' name.

- We release _____ and (Insert the name of parents) _____ from every ungodly parental linkage, in the name of Jesus.

- Lord Jesus, manifest Yourself in their lives by Your name called 'Wonderful.'

- Father, we declare, like David, _____ and (Insert the name of parents) _____ will fulfill God's plan for their lives, in their generations and speak of Your marvelous work in their lives, in Jesus' name. WE AGREE!

    #_____ speaks

DAY 30

SCRIPTURE MEDITATION

1. *But the manifestation of the Spirit is given to every man to profit withal. [1Co 12:7 KJV]*

CONFESSIONS

- We decree that the bloodline of Jesus began in heaven, was poured out through Jesus on the altar of Calvary and returned upward to heaven again on the 3rd day. Jesus arose triumphant over death, hell and the grave and carried His own precious blood into the heavenly Holy of Holies where it was accepted for man. The resurrected Lamb of God closed the circle by giving glory to God the Father. The powerful, redemptive Blood is returned to its heavenly terminal and there, before the throne of the Living God, the Blood ever speaks mercy for man...and mercy for (Insert name). (Heb 12:24)

- Every spirit of death assigned against _____ and _____, destinies is canceled in the name of Jesus.

- We withdraw their progress from every satanic regulation and domination, in the name of Jesus.

- Father, we declare, like David, _____ and (Insert the name of parents) _____ will fulfill God's plan for their lives, in their generations and speak of Your marvelous work in their lives, in Jesus' name. WE AGREE!

#_____speaks

DAY 31

SCRIPTURE MEDITATION

1. *On the next day much people that were come to the feast, when they heard that Jesus was coming to Jerusalem, [Jhn 12:12 KJV]*

CONFESSIONS

- Lord, we draw a bloodline that the enemy cannot cross around, _____ my family, bloodline, descendants, inheritance, possessions, lands, territories, birthrights, promises, prophecies, and all that You have given us stewardship over, in Jesus' Name.

- Every garment of darkness is roasted by the fire of God, in the name of Jesus.

- We declare that _____ and (Insert the name of parents) _____ will not live a floating life, in the name of Jesus.

- Every deeply entrenched problem in their lives, dry to the roots, in the name of Jesus.

- Father, we declare, like David, _____ and (Insert the name of parents) _____ will fulfill God's plan for their lives, in their generations and speak of Your marvelous work in their lives, in Jesus' name. WE AGREE!

#_____speaks

DAY 32

SCRIPTURE MEDITATION

1. *And when Paul had gathered a bundle of sticks, and laid [them] on the fire, there came a viper out of the heat, and fastened on his hand. 4 And when the barbarians saw the [venomous] beast hang on his hand, they said among themselves, No doubt this man is a murderer, whom, though he hath escaped the sea, yet vengeance suffereth not to live. 5 And he shook off the beast into the fire, and felt no harm. [Act 28:3-5 KJV]*

CONFESSIONS

- We decree that the same power that raised Jesus from the dead lives in _____.

- Every stronghold and cycle of failure is broken, in Jesus' name.

- Every internal warfare in _____ and (Insert the name of parents) _____ lives is quenched, in the name of Jesus.

- Every internal thief be exposed, in the name of Jesus.

- Anything planted in _____ and (Insert the name of parents) _____ past that would hinder their future, come out with all your roots and tentacles, in the name of Jesus.

- Father, we declare, like David, _____ and (Insert the name of parents) _____ will fulfill God's plan for their lives, in their generations and speak of Your marvelous work in their lives, in Jesus' name. **WE AGREE!**

#_____speaks

DAY 33

Scripture Meditation

1. *Jesus saith unto her, Said I not unto thee, that, if thou wouldest believe, thou shouldest see the glory of God? Then they took away the stone [from the place] where the dead was laid. And Jesus lifted up [his] eyes, and said, Father, I thank thee that thou hast heard me. And I knew that thou hearest me always: but because of the people which stand by I said [it], that they may believe that thou hast sent me. And when he thus had spoken, he cried with a loud voice, Lazarus, come forth. And he that was dead came forth, bound hand and foot with graveclothes: and his face was bound about with a napkin. Jesus saith unto them, Loose him, and let him go. [Jhn 11:40-44 KJV]*

Confessions

- We speak life and release the resurrection power of Christ over, upon, and into every cell, fiber, molecule and strand of RNA and DNA of _____ _____existence in Jesus' name!

- Let the handwriting of household wickedness be erased off of _____ and (Insert the name of parents) _____lives, in the name of Jesus.

- Destiny thieves that have stolen their divine deposits, return them now, in the name of Jesus.

- Father, we declare, like David, _____ and (Insert the name of parents) _____ will fulfill God's plan for their lives, in their generations and speak of Your marvelous work in their lives, in Jesus' name. WE AGREE!

    #_____speaks

DAY 34

SCRIPTURE MEDITATION

1. *And when Paul had laid [his] hands upon them, the Holy Ghost came on them; and they spake with tongues, and prophesied. [Act 19:6 KJV]*

CONFESSIONS

- We release life and resurrection power to infuse every dead, dull, dry and lifeless dream, goal, passion, prophecy, and pursuit that God has determined for __ _____ and (Insert the name of parents) ___ _____, in Jesus' Name!

- We declare _____ and (Insert the name of parents) _____ receive explosive breakthroughs through the power of the Spirit; We reject every false and counterfeit breakthrough, in the name of Jesus.

- Lord, change _____ and (Insert the name of parents) _____ destiny to the best.

- We cancel every evil power struggling to re-program _____ and (Insert the name of parents) ___ _____ lives, in the name of Jesus.

- Father, we declare, like David, _____ and (Insert the name of parents) _____ will fulfill God's plan for their lives, in their generations and speak of Your marvelous work in their lives, in Jesus' name. **WE AGREE!**

#_____speaks

DAY 35

Scripture Meditation

1. *And at midnight Paul and Silas prayed, and sang praises unto God: and the prisoners heard them. And suddenly there was a great earthquake, so that the foundations of the prison were shaken: and immediately all the doors were opened, and every one's bands were loosed. [Act 16:25-26 KJV]*

Confessions

- We release the Blood of Jesus to quicken and activate our faith to rise and our hope to awaken in, Jesus' name!

- We thank the Lord Jesus for scattering the enemies of _____ and (Insert the name of parents) _____ divine destinies.

- Every organ in _____ and (Insert the name of parents) _____ bodies is washed by the Blood of Jesus.

- Every ungodly spiritual parent is released now, in Jesus' name.

- Father, we declare, like David, _____ and (Insert the name of parents) _____ will fulfill God's plan for their lives, in their generations and speak of Your marvelous work in their lives, in Jesus' name. **WE AGREE!**

#_____speaks

DAY 36

Scripture Meditation

1. *Finally, my brethren, be strong in the Lord, and in the power of his might. Put on the whole armour of God, that ye may be able to stand against the wiles of the devil. For we wrestle not against flesh and blood, but against principalities, against powers, against the rulers of the darkness of this world, against spiritual wickedness in high [places]. Wherefore take unto you the whole armour of God, that ye may be able to withstand in the evil day, and having done all, to stand. Stand therefore, having your loins girt about with truth, and having on the breastplate of righteousness; And your feet shod with the preparation of the gospel of peace; Above all, taking the shield of faith, wherewith ye shall be able to quench all the fiery darts of the wicked. And take the helmet of salvation, and the sword of the Spirit, which is the word of God: Praying always with all prayer and supplication in the Spirit, and watching thereunto with all perseverance and supplication for all saints; [Eph 6:10-18 KJV]*

Confessions

- We decree the name of Jesus is victorious over disability, sickness, infirmity, and disease in _____ _____ body!

- Every unprofitable love targeted against ____ ___and (Insert the name of parents) _____ ___, is broken now, in the name of Jesus.

- Every stubborn curse is broken by fire, in Jesus' name.

- We break every evil clock controlling _____ ___ and (Insert the name of parents) _____ lives on the wall of fire, in the name of Jesus.

- Father, we thank you for answering prayer!
- Father, we declare, like David, _____ and (Insert the name of parents) _____ will fulfill God's plan for their lives, in their generations and speak of Your marvelous work in their lives, in Jesus' name. **WE AGREE!**

#_____speaks

DAY 37

SCRIPTURE MEDITATION/CONFESSIONS

1. *Thine, O LORD, [is] the greatness, and the power, and the glory, and the victory, and the majesty: for all [that is] in the heaven and in the earth [is thine]; thine [is] the kingdom, O LORD, and thou art exalted as head above all, in _____ and (Insert the name of parents) _____, in Jesus' name. WE AGREE! [1Ch 29:11 KJV]*

2. *For the LORD your God [is] he that goeth with you, to fight for _____ and (Insert the name of parents) _____ against our enemies, to save them. [Deu 20:4 KJV]*

#_____speaks

DAY 38

Scripture Meditation

1. *[[A Psalm.]] O sing unto the LORD a new song; for he hath done marvelous things: his right hand, and his holy arm, hath gotten him the victory. [Psa 98:1 KJV]*

Confessions

- Father, we declare the song of the Lord is released through _____ and (Insert the name of parents) _____ that you have done marvelous things and that your right hand and your holy arm have gotten them the victory, in Jesus' name.

- We decree that Jesus has already taken up _____ _____ disabilities, infirmities, and diseases upon the cross and by your stripes and blood; we declare _____ _____ is healed, in Jesus' name. WE AGREE!

    #_____speaks

DAY 39

Scripture Meditation

1. *But thanks [be] to God, which giveth us the victory through our Lord Jesus Christ. [1Co 15:57 KJV]*

Confessions

- Thanks be to God, who has given us the victory concerning _____, through our Lord Jesus Christ.
- Lord, cleanse and filter bloodline, through the power that is in the name, and Blood of Jesus. WE AGREE!

#_____speaks

DAY 40

SCRIPTURE MEDITATION

Acts 2:1-16

1. And when the day of Pentecost was fully come, they were all with one accord in one place.

2. And suddenly there came a sound from heaven as of a rushing mighty wind, and it filled the entire house where they were sitting.

3. And there **appeared unto them cloven tongues like as of fire, and it sat upon each of them**.

4. **And they (and _____) were all filled with the Holy Ghost, and began to speak with other tongues, as the Spirit gave them utterance.**

5. And there were dwelling at Jerusalem Jews, devout men, out of every nation under heaven.

6. Now when this was noised abroad, the multitude came together, and were confounded, because that **every man heard them speak in his own language**. We decree that we will hear _____ **speak in his own language.**

7. And they were all amazed and marveled, saying one to another, Behold, are not all these which speak Galileans?

8. And how hear we every man in our own tongue, wherein we were born?

9. Parthians, and Medes, and Elamites, and the dwellers in Mesopotamia, and in Judaea, and Cappadocia, in Pontus, and Asia,

10. Phrygia, and Pamphylia, in Egypt, and in the parts of

Libya about Cyrene, and strangers of Rome, Jews and proselytes, Cretes and Arabians, **we do hear them and _____speak in our tongues the wonderful works of God.**

11. And they were all amazed, and were in doubt, saying one to another, What meaneth this?

12. Others mocking said, These men are full of new wine.

13. But Peter, standing up with the eleven, lifted up his voice, and said unto them, Ye men of Judaea, and all [ye] that dwell at Jerusalem, be this known unto you, and hearken to my words:

14. For these are not drunken, as ye suppose, seeing it is [but] the third hour of the day.

15. But this is that which was spoken by the prophet Joel; **And it shall come to pass in the last days, saith God, I will pour out of my Spirit upon all flesh: and your sons and your daughters and _____ shall prophesy, and your young men shall see visions, and your old men shall dream dreams:**

16. **And on my servants and on my handmaidens, and on _____I will pour out in those days of my Spirit; and they shall prophesy:**

17. And I will shew wonders in heaven above, and signs in the earth beneath; blood, and fire, and vapour of smoke:

18. The sun shall be turned into darkness, and the moon into blood, before that great and notable day of the Lord come:

19. **And it shall come to pass, [that] _____ and (Insert the name of parents) _____ shall call on the name of the Lord shall be saved.** Act 2:1-21 KJV

CONFESSIONS

- Father, as we come to the end of this fast, but not the end of our expectation. We trust and believe that You have heard us. This is the confidence that we have in You, that if we ask anything according to Your will, You hear us, and if You hear us, we know that we have the petitions that we ask. (1 John 5:14)
- Then shall my enemies turn back in the day that I cry out; this I know, for God is for me. (Psalm 56:9)
- **Finally, we declare and call as witnesses Heaven and Earth,**
    - _____ speaks with tongues of fire.
    - _____ not only speaks his/her native language, but he/she speaks with other tongues as the Spirit gives him/her utterance.
    - _____ speaks the wonderful works of God.
    - _____ prophesies the Word of the Lord.
    - _____ sees visions and dreams and **speaks** them forth to the glory of God, in Jesus' name. WE AGREE!

#_____speaks

APPENDIX

Resources

Ages 0-3

1. If you are concerned about your child's development and want to track milestones or check to see if there is an issue to be concerned about, look at the Center for Disease Control's Learn the Signs: Act Early website, found here:
https://www.cdc.gov/ncbddd/actearly/index.html

    There is also an app available on their website you can download for free which helps to track milestones.

2. Here is another resource about concerns regarding your child's development:
https://www.dds.ca.gov/EarlyStart/docs/ReasonsForConcern_English.pdf

3. If you are a parent of an infant or toddler and have concerns related to speech development, cognitive development, gross/fine motor skills, adaptive skills, or behavioral functioning, you can reach out to the Regional Center (which is a non-profit, private corporations which contract with the state of California's Department of Developmental Services) which serves individuals with disabilities and provides services for free to families. There are Regional Centers across California, which are particular to each geographic area, and are accessible to anyone. This link allows you to look up the contact information for the Regional Center specific to your area:
https://www.dds.ca.gov/rc/RCList.cfm

This link gives more information about them: https://www.dds.ca.gov/RC/

4. You can also contact your medical provider if you have any concerns related to your child's development, and they should make a referral for you to the appropriate specialist within your medical network, or they will refer you to your local Regional Center or school district. If your medical provider denies services (for speech therapy for example), then the Regional Center is your next best place to call because they pick up where medical providers don't provide services.

Ages 3 and up

5. Your local school district has responsibility for child find (meaning finding and serving students with suspected disabilities). If you have any questions/concerns related to your child's development (including for speech, gross/fine motor skills, adaptive skills, cognitive development, or behavioral/social-emotional development) you can contact your local school district and request an evaluation. Simply call the special education department, or the school in your neighborhood, or if they have a separate preschool program and that is appropriate for the age of your child, you can contact them as well.

6. You can also access information about these services at the California Department of Education, Special Education division, website:

California Department of Education Special Education Division 1430 N Street, Suite 2401, Sacramento, CA 95814 I 916-445-4613 I http://www.cde.ca.gov/sp/se

7. If you have difficulties accessing services or navigating the system, you can contact this organization for help: *www.disabilityrightsca.org*

8. Websites with helpful information about Autism:
    a. www.captain.ca.gov
    b. www.autismspeaks.com
    c. www.dds.ca.gov
    d. https://health.ucdavis.edu/mindinstitute/ Information from the UC Davis MIND Institute
    e. **HealthyChildren.org** AAP parenting website backed by pediatricians. Site includes everything from general child health guidance to information on specific issues and conditions.
    f. https://www.nationalautismcenter.org

9. African American Developmental Disability Parent Alliance Group (AADDPA) has a Facebook page you can access. This group does not just focus on autism, but autism is included.

FREE TRAINING FOR FAMILIES:

10. You can get free information/training on autism and how to support your child at home utilizing these resources (you only have to use your email address to create an account-they never use your personal information): https://afirm.fpg.unc.edu

11.

12. https://autisminternetmodules.org

13. https://asdtoddler.fpg.unc.edu

14. https://health.ucdavis.edu/mindinstitute/centers/cedd/cedd_adept.html

ABOUT THE AUTHOR

KARLA ALLEN has spent her life in Jesus Christ helping to facilitate individuals in discovering God's original intent for their lives. She is a dynamic motivational/inspirational speaker, teacher, author, and coach. Her previous works include *Conversations of a Watchman* prayer book and *Show Me Your Glory* from the *Song Chronicles*. Karla is the founder and president of Fresh Reign Publishing (www.freshreign.com), which exists to create a passion within the authors, and readers for an intimate relationship with Jesus Christ. The ultimate goal of Fresh Reign is to assist one to increase one's capacity to hear the voice of the Holy Spirit and to leave a legacy of the reign of Jesus Christ.

Over the years, Karla has also served students of diverse socioeconomic, academic, and cultural backgrounds. As a devoted educator in the public-school system, Karla has fused her educational and experiential knowledge to emerge as a positive role model for students, trustworthy spiritual leader to leaders and reliable mentor to up-and-coming leaders. Through the foundational beliefs of building relationships, respect for others, and personal accountability, Karla imparts fresh ideas for transformation and reinvention for the next generation.

www.ingramcontent.com/pod-product-compliance
Lightning Source LLC
Chambersburg PA
CBHW060818050426
42449CB00008B/1711